VET

by Marne Ventura

a Capstone company — publishers for children

Raintree is an imprint of Capstone Global Library Limited, a company incorporated in England and Wales having its registered office at 264 Banbury Road, Oxford, OX2 7DY – Registered company number: 6695582

www.raintree.co.uk
myorders@raintree.co.uk

Text © Capstone Global Library Limited 2020
The moral rights of the proprietor have been asserted.

All rights reserved. No part of this publication may be reproduced in any form or by any means (including photocopying or storing it in any medium by electronic means and whether or not transiently or incidentally to some other use of this publication) without the written permission of the copyright owner, except in accordance with the provisions of the Copyright, Designs and Patents Act 1988 or under the terms of a licence issued by the Copyright Licensing Agency, Barnard's Inn, 86 Fetter Lane, London, EC4A 1EN (www.cla.co.uk). Applications for the copyright owner's written permission should be addressed to the publisher.
Printed and bound in India.

Editor: Mirella Miller
Designer: Becky Daum
Production Specialist: Ryan Gale

ISBN 978 1 4747 7471 0 (hardback)
ISBN 978 1 4747 8125 1 (paperback)

British Library Cataloguing in Publication Data
A full catalogue record for this book is available from the British Library

Acknowledgements
iStockphoto: andresr, 17, BartCo, 26–27, BraunS, 30–31, kali9, 5, 10–11, 18–19, 28, Mypurgatoryyears, 14–15, ptaxa, 12–13, SashaFoxWalters, 25, SelectStock, cover, zilli, 13
Shutterstock Images: belizar, 6–7, ChameleonsEye, 9, David Tadevosian, 22–23, Deborah Kolb, 21

Every effort has been made to contact copyright holders of material reproduced in this book. Any omissions will be rectified in subsequent printings if notice is given to the publisher.

All the internet addresses (URLs) given in this book were valid at the time of going to press. However, due to the dynamic nature of the internet, some addresses may have changed, or sites may have changed or ceased to exist since publication. While the author and publisher regret any inconvenience this may cause readers, no responsibility for any such changes can be accepted by either the author or the publisher.

CONTENTS

CHAPTER ONE
WHAT A VET DOES............ 4

CHAPTER TWO
QUALITIES AND SKILLS 8

CHAPTER THREE
SCHOOL FOR VETS............ 16

CHAPTER FOUR
GETTING EXPERIENCE 20

CHAPTER FIVE
WHERE VETS WORK 24

Glossary 28
Other jobs to consider 29
Activity 30
Find out more 32
Index 32

CHAPTER 1

WHAT A VET DOES

Animals are important to people in many ways. Pets are friends. Service dogs help people. Farmers raise animals for food. Sometimes animals get hurt or sick. They are taken to a vet, or veterinarian. A vet is an animal doctor.

Vets **treat** sick animals. They care for hurt animals. They give animals **vaccines**. They operate when an animal needs surgery.

Vets give animals regular check-ups to make sure they are healthy.

Vets work with all kinds of animals. People bring pets to a veterinary **clinic**. Vets visit animals in zoos and help the wild animals there. Vets also go to farms. They make sure animals raised for food stay healthy. Vets also treat animals used in sports. These include racehorses and racing dogs.

Do you like taking care of animals? Maybe a job as a vet is for you.

Vets look after a maned wolf puppy at a zoo.

7

CHAPTER 2

QUALITIES AND Skills

Vets like working with many kinds of animals. They care for cats and dogs. They also help birds, lizards and snakes. Some might treat cows or horses. Others help zoo animals such as tigers or giraffes.

A zoo vet handles an injured koala.

Vets have a big job. Owners trust them with their animals' health. Vets are caring. They feel comfortable around animals. Vets need to work well with people too. Vets tell owners how to care for their animals. They explain what is wrong when an animal is sick or hurt. They help owners as well as animals.

Good vets work well with both people and animals.

The animals that vets work with may have sharp teeth or claws.

Some baby animals drink milk from a bottle.

Working with animals can be hard. A puppy might not stay still. A bird might bite. A cat might scratch. Lions and tigers can hurt people. Vets need to be brave and strong. They also need to be careful.

The animal's fur is shaved when the vet performs surgery on it.

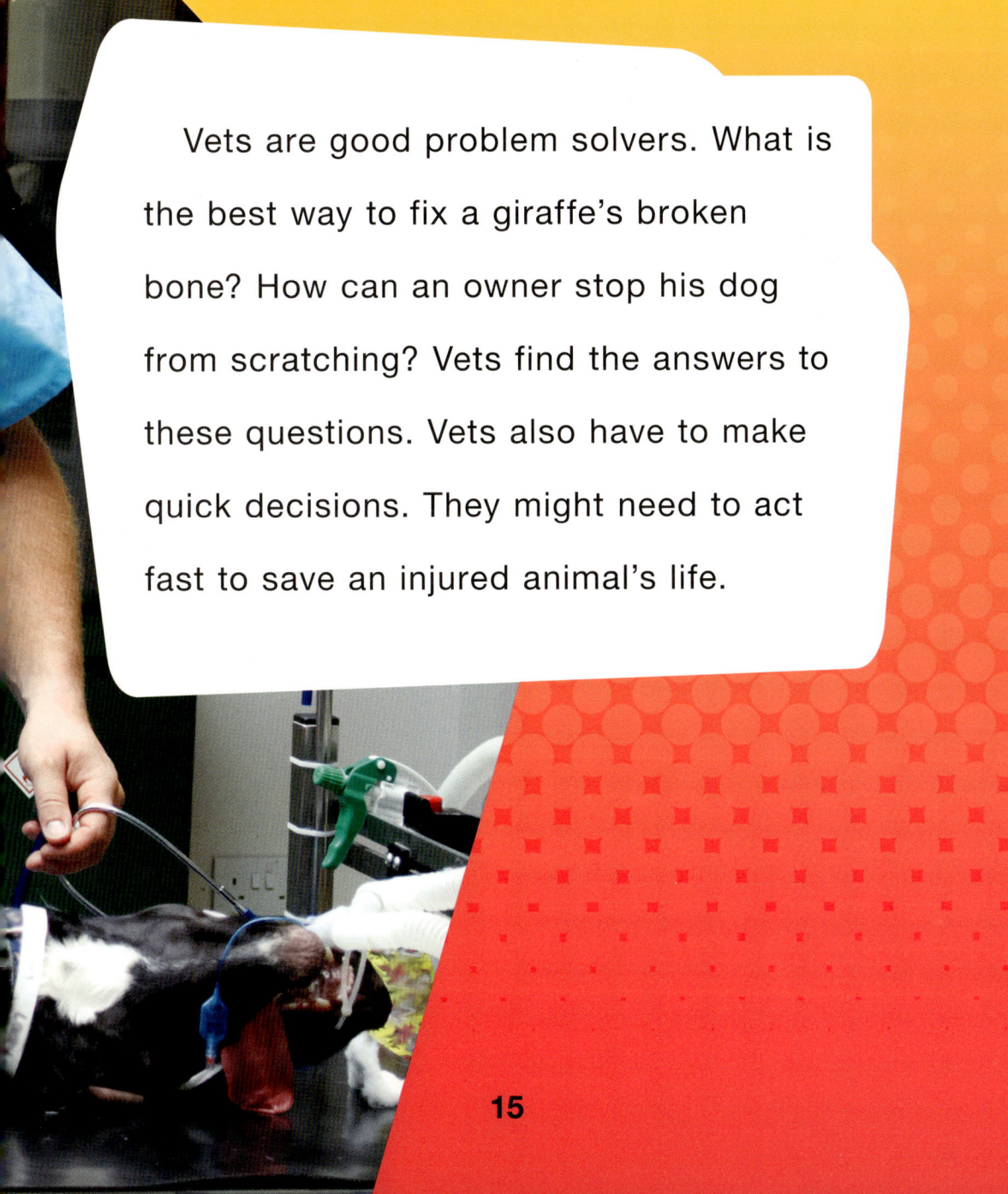

Vets are good problem solvers. What is the best way to fix a giraffe's broken bone? How can an owner stop his dog from scratching? Vets find the answers to these questions. Vets also have to make quick decisions. They might need to act fast to save an injured animal's life.

CHAPTER 3

SCHOOL FOR Vets

To become a vet, students need to get good grades at GCSE and A level. Then they need to study for five or six years for a **degree** in veterinary science at university.

There are eight universities across the UK that offer veterinary science degrees.

Vet students learn about the body parts of different animals.

Would you like to be a vet? You can start learning now. Get good grades in school. Take lots of maths and science classes. Read books about animals. Watch TV shows about animals. Visit the zoo.

COLLEGE COURSES

Some colleges have courses for jobs with animals. These prepare students to be vet technicians, nurses and assistants.

Find out if there are any clubs or activities about science and animals near your home.

CHAPTER 4

GETTING Experience

It takes a lot of practice to be a vet. Any work with animals helps. There are many ways to get this experience. Some families have pets. Taking care of a pet is good experience for a future vet.

Maybe a friend or neighbour needs help. Take a friend's dog for a walk. Play with and feed the neighbours' cat while they are away.

Dog walking is an easy way to get experience with animals.

Some pet shelters need **volunteers**. These volunteers help feed the animals. They clean animals' homes. They give the animals attention. They play with the animals. Some zoos and wild animal parks have volunteer programmes too.

CHARITIES

People can help animals in other ways. Organizations such as the Blue Cross and the Battersea Dogs and Cats Home need help with raising funds. They also get help from volunteers.

Many animal shelters depend on volunteers to take care of the animals.

CHAPTER 5

WHERE Vets Work

Vets work in many places. Most vets work in veterinary clinics. They help pets such as dogs, cats and birds.

Other vets go to animals' homes. They might go to a dairy farm to help cows. They might visit a zoo to care for a sick tiger. They might go to a racetrack to check on a horse.

Vets can focus on equine practice, which is the care of horses.

Some vets work in **laboratories**. They do research. They study ways to better care for animals. Other vets work in the universities teaching veterinary science. They help others become vets.

A vet teaches students about how to care for sheep.

UNDER OATH

When students become vets, they make a promise. It is called the Veterinary **Oath**. Vets promise to help animals.

Becoming a vet is a popular career choice among children. Vets earn between £25,000 and £48,000 per year on average. Although it pays well the working hours are long.

GLOSSARY

animal science
study of animals that are under the control of humans

clinic
place to get medical care

degree
academic award given to students after they complete a course of study

laboratory
place where scientists do research

oath
promise

treat
give medical care to

vaccine
medicine given to prevent illness

volunteer
someone who works without pay

OTHER JOBS TO CONSIDER

VETERINARY NURSE

Nurses take care of the animals at clinics. They give the animals medicine or give them medical tests. They also prepare animals for operations and clean up afterwards.

VETERINARY CARE ASSISTANT

Assistants work alongside the vets and veterinary nurses to give nursing care for the animals. They exercise, groom and feed animals who are staying at the clinic. They answer phone calls and give advice on health care.

ACTIVITY

BECOMING A VET

Not sure if a career as a vet is for you? Here are some activities to help you decide. First, read books from your library about being a vet. Then make two lists. The first is a list of what you would like about being a vet. The second is a list about what you might not like.

Consider talking to a vet about the job. See if you can arrange a time to meet with the vet. Make a list of questions ahead of time. If you have a pet, you can also go along on a vet visit. You can see what the vet is like in action. Watch as he or she takes care of your pet. What qualities does he or she have?

FIND OUT MORE

Interested in becoming a vet? Learn more here:

Books
Vet Academy: Are you ready for the challenge? Steve Martin (Ivy Kids, 2017)
Vet (Here to Help), James Nixon (Franklin Watts, 2019)

Websites
British Veterinary Association website: advice on how to become a vet
www.bva.co.uk/Professional-development/Careers/Becoming-a-vet/
National Careers Service: government guidelines on how to become a vet
nationalcareers.service.gov.uk/job-profiles/vet

INDEX

animal science 16, 26
clinics 6, 24
degrees 16
experience 20
farms 6, 25

laboratories 26
pay 27
pet owners 11, 15
pets 4, 6, 20, 22, 24
schools 17–18, 26
surgery 5
universities 16, 17, 26

vaccines 5
Veterinary Oath 27
volunteers 22
zoos 6, 8, 18, 22, 25